W9-BAH-714

Healthy Living
Exercise
by Vanessa Black
Bullfrog
Books

Ideas for Parents and Teachers

Bullfrog Books let children practice reading informational text at the earliest reading levels. Repetition, familiar words, and photo labels support early readers.

Before Reading

- Discuss the cover photo. What does it tell them?
- Look at the picture glossary together. Read and discuss the words.

Read the Book

- "Walk" through the book and look at the photos. Let the child ask questions. Point out the photo labels.
- Read the book to the child, or have him or her read independently.

After Reading

- Prompt the child to think more. Ask: How much exercise do you think you get a day? What is your favorite physical activity?

Bullfrog Books are published by Jump!
5357 Penn Avenue South
Minneapolis, MN 55419
www.jumplibrary.com

Library of Congress Cataloging-in-Publication Data

Names: Black, Vanessa, author.
Title: Exercise / by Vanessa Black.
Description: Minneapolis, MN: Jump!, Inc. [2017]
Series: Healthy living | "Bullfrog Books are published by Jump!." | Audience: Ages 5–8.
Audience: K to grade 3.
Includes bibliographical references and index.
Identifiers: LCCN 2016029368 (print)
LCCN 2016031891 (ebook)
ISBN 9781620315439 (hardcover: alk. paper)
ISBN 9781620315835 (pbk.)
ISBN 9781624964916 (ebook)
Subjects: LCSH: Exercise—Juvenile literature.
Health—Juvenile literature.
Classification: LCC RA781 .B537 2017 (print)
LCC RA781 (ebook) | DDC 613.7/1—dc23
LC record available at https://lccn.loc.gov/2016029368

Editor: Jenny Fretland VanVoorst
Book Designer: Molly Ballanger
Photo Researcher: Molly Ballanger

Photo Credits: All photos by Shutterstock except: Alamy, 8–9, 12; iStock, 6–7, 16–17; Thinkstock, 14–15, 18, 23tl.

Printed in the United States of America at Corporate Graphics in North Mankato, Minnesota.

Table of Contents

Get Fit!

Mara and
Zed run.

They jump.
They swim.

Exercise is good for you.
It helps you stay healthy.

Noah bikes.
His muscles work.
They get strong.

Rory is in a bad mood.

He shoots hoops.

Soon he feels better.

Beth plays tennis with Henry.

She is having fun.

She is losing weight.

Jacinda kicks.

She punches.

She does karate.

She can keep herself safe.

Roberto plays soccer.
He runs.
His heart pumps fast.
It helps him sleep well.

Swim. Hike.
Jump. Play.

Try a lot of things.
See what you like best.

Exercise is fun!
Do it every day.

Your Daily Exercise

You should be active at least 60 minutes every day.

stretch
Stretch before and after exercise. It helps keep your muscles safe and free from injury.

drink water
It is very important that you drink water before, during, and after exercise. Your muscles need water to work.

warm up
Before you play hard, it is good to let your muscles warm up. One good way to warm up is to take a short jog.

snack healthfully
Before and after exercise it is good to have a healthful snack, like a protein bar, a piece of fruit, or a hard-boiled egg.

Picture Glossary

karate
A form of fighting that uses kicks and punches for both exercise and self-defense.

muscles
The parts of the body that help you move.

mood
How you feel.

tennis
A game in which players use rackets to hit a ball back and forth across a low net.

Index

To Learn More

Learning more is as easy as 1, 2, 3.

1) Go to www.factsurfer.com

2) Enter "exercise" into the search box.

3) Click the "Surf" button to see a list of websites.

With factsurfer.com, finding more information is just a click away.